EASY INSULIN RESISTANCE DIET PLAN COOKBOOK 2023

Delicious, Simple And Nutritious Recipes Guide To Help Lose Weight Fast, Fight Or Reduce Inflammation And Lower Blood Sugar Levels

Dr Miles Jones

Table Of Contents

Introduction

Once upon a time, in a small town, there lived a passionate writer named Emily. Emily had always dreamed of creating a book that would not only captivate readers but also inspire them to lead healthier lives. One day, while researching a topic for her new book, she stumbled upon the "Insulin Resistance Diet Plan Cookbook."

Intrigued, Emily delved into the book, discovering a wealth of knowledge about managing insulin resistance through proper nutrition. The cookbook not only provided delicious recipes but also explained the science behind the condition and how certain foods could help regulate blood sugar levels.

Emily was astounded by the impact of the cookbook on her own health and well-being. Inspired by her newfound knowledge, she decided to incorporate the Insulin Resistance Diet Plan Cookbook into her own book. She carefully crafted a chapter, sharing her personal experiences and the positive changes she had witnessed.

As Emily's book reached the shelves, readers were drawn to her authentic storytelling and insightful advice. Many found solace in her relatable journey and were inspired to make positive changes in their own lives.

Thanks to the "Insulin Resistance Diet Plan Cookbook," Emily's book became a testament to the power of knowledge, personal growth, and the ability to inspire others to embrace healthier lifestyles.

By reading Emily's book, readers were able to reap numerous benefits. Firstly, they gained a comprehensive understanding of insulin resistance and its impact on their health. The book provided clear explanations, breaking down complex concepts into easily understandable terms.

Secondly, readers learned about the importance of proper nutrition in managing insulin resistance. The Insulin Resistance Diet Plan Cookbook offered a wide range of delicious recipes that were specifically designed to help regulate blood sugar levels and promote overall wellness. By following these recipes, readers could make positive changes to their diet and experience improved energy levels, weight management, and better control over their blood sugar.

Moreover, Emily's book served as a source of inspiration and motivation. Through her personal journey, readers realized that they were not alone in their struggles with insulin resistance. They gained confidence in their ability to make positive changes and were motivated to adopt a healthier lifestyle.

Ultimately, the book empowered readers with the knowledge and tools necessary to take control of their health. It served as a valuable resource, equipping them with practical strategies and delicious recipes to manage insulin resistance effectively. Through Emily's book, readers discovered a path to better health, renewed hope, and the opportunity to live a fulfilling life.

Insulin Resistance And PCOS

The pancreas secretes the hormone insulin, which aids in controlling blood glucose (sugar) levels.

On the other hand, PCOS itself can exacerbate insulin resistance. The presence of excess androgens in PCOS can further impair insulin sensitivity, creating a vicious cycle. Insulin resistance leads to higher insulin levels, which in turn stimulate the ovaries to produce more androgens, perpetuating the hormonal imbalance and insulin resistance. This cycle can contribute to the development of other metabolic abnormalities, such as dyslipidemia (abnormal blood lipid levels) and hypertension (high blood pressure), increasing the risk of cardiovascular disease.

The diagnosis of insulin resistance and PCOS involves a comprehensive evaluation of symptoms, medical history, physical examination, and laboratory tests. Blood tests are used to measure fasting glucose and insulin levels, as well as other markers of insulin resistance, such as glycated hemoglobin (HbA1c) and triglyceride levels. Additionally, an ultrasound examination of the ovaries may be performed to assess the presence of cysts and other structural abnormalities.

The management of insulin resistance and PCOS involves a multifaceted approach aimed at improving insulin sensitivity, reducing symptoms, and minimizing the risk of long-term complications. Lifestyle modifications form the cornerstone of treatment and include regular exercise, a balanced diet rich in whole grains, lean proteins, and vegetables, and weight management for those who are overweight or obese. Medications such as metformin, which improves insulin sensitivity and regulates blood sugar levels, may be prescribed to manage insulin resistance and its associated metabolic abnormalities. Oral contraceptives or anti-androgen medications may also be used to regulate menstrual cycles, reduce excessive hair growth, and improve acne in women with PCOS.

Living Well To Eat well

Living Well to Eat Well:

Living well to eat well encompasses adopting a holistic approach to managing insulin resistance. It involves making lifestyle changes, including dietary modifications, physical activity, stress management, and sufficient sleep. By incorporating these elements into daily life, individuals can improve insulin sensitivity, regulate blood sugar levels, and enhance overall well-being.

Insulin Resistance Diet Plan:

A well-designed insulin resistance diet plan focuses on controlling carbohydrate intake, choosing the right types of carbohydrates, consuming adequate protein and healthy fats, and emphasizing nutrient-dense foods. Here are some essential guidelines to bear in mind:

Carbohydrate Management:

Limit refined carbohydrates and added sugars: These include white bread, pasta, pastries, sugary beverages, and processed snacks. They cause rapid spikes in blood sugar levels, contributing to insulin resistance.

Choose complex carbohydrates: Opt for whole grains like brown rice, quinoa, and whole wheat bread, which have a lower glycemic index and provide sustained energy.

Portion control: Monitor carbohydrate servings to maintain stable blood sugar levels. Consult with a registered dietitian to determine an appropriate daily carbohydrate intake based on individual needs.

Protein and Healthy Fats:

Include lean protein sources: Examples include poultry, fish, tofu, legumes, and low-fat dairy products. Protein encourages satiety, improves muscle health, and aids in blood sugar regulation.

Consume healthy fats: Include sources such as avocados, nuts, seeds, olive oil, and fatty fish like salmon. These provide essential fatty acids, promote heart health, and aid in insulin sensitivity.

Emphasize Nutrient-Dense Foods:

Increase vegetable intake: Incorporate a variety of non-starchy vegetables like leafy greens, cruciferous vegetables, peppers, and tomatoes. They are rich in fiber, vitamins, minerals, and antioxidants.

Choose low-glycemic fruits: Opt for berries, cherries, apples, and pears, which have a lower impact on blood sugar levels compared to tropical fruits or fruit juices.

Prioritize fiber-rich foods: Whole grains, legumes, vegetables, and fruits are excellent sources of dietary fiber, which slows down digestion, stabilizes blood sugar, and promotes gut health.

Other Considerations:

Stay hydrated: Drink plenty of water throughout the day to support overall health and assist in maintaining stable blood sugar levels.

Regular physical activity: Engage in aerobic exercises, resistance training, or other forms of physical activity to improve insulin sensitivity, manage weight, and boost overall well-being.

Stress management and sleep: Incorporate stress-reduction techniques like meditation, yoga, or deep breathing. Prioritize adequate sleep, as poor sleep quality can affect insulin sensitivity and blood

Breakfast

Berry Quinoa Parfait:
Ingredients:

- ☐ 1 cup cooked quinoa
- ☐ 1 cup mixed berries (blueberries, raspberries, strawberries)
- ☐ 1/4 cup unsweetened almond milk
- ☐ 1 tablespoon chia seeds
- ☐ 1 tablespoon chopped nuts (almonds, walnuts)
- ☐ 1 teaspoon honey (optional)

Instructions:

1. In a bowl, layer cooked quinoa, mixed berries, and chia seeds.
2. Pour almond milk over the layers.
3. Top with chopped nuts and drizzle with honey if desired.
4. Mix well before consuming. The combination of high-fiber quinoa and antioxidant-rich berries will provide sustained energy and help stabilize blood sugar levels.

Veggie Omelet:
Ingredients:

- ☐ 2 eggs

- 1/4 cup chopped bell peppers
- 1/4 cup chopped spinach
- 1/4 cup diced tomatoes
- 1 tablespoon olive oil
- Salt and pepper to taste

Instructions:
1. Beat the eggs in a bowl and season with salt and pepper.
2. In a non-stick pan, warm up the olive oil over medium heat.
3. Add bell peppers, spinach, and tomatoes to the pan and sauté until slightly softened.
4. Before the omelet sets, pour the beaten eggs over the vegetables.
5. Flip the omelet and cook for another minute until fully cooked.
6. Serve hot, as this protein-packed breakfast will provide essential nutrients while keeping blood sugar levels stable.

Almond Flour Pancakes:
Ingredients:
- 1 cup almond flour
- 2 tablespoons coconut flour
- 1/2 teaspoon baking powder

- 1/4 teaspoon cinnamon
- 2 eggs
- 1/4 cup unsweetened almond milk
- 1 tablespoon coconut oil (for cooking)
- Sugar-free syrup (optional)

Instructions:

1. In a bowl, mix almond flour, coconut flour, baking powder, and cinnamon.
2. In a separate bowl, whisk eggs and almond milk until well combined.
3. The ingredients should be combined and mixed thoroughly to create a smooth batter.
4. Heat coconut oil in a non-stick pan over medium heat.
5. Pour 1/4 cup of the batter onto the pan and spread it into a round shape.
6. Cook until bubbles form on the surface, then flip and cook the other side.
7. Repeat with the remaining batter.
8. Serve the pancakes with sugar-free syrup, if desired. These pancakes are low in carbohydrates and high in healthy fats, making them suitable for an insulin resistance diet.

Greek Yogurt Parfait:

Ingredients:

- ☐ 1 cup Greek yogurt (unsweetened)
- ☐ 1/4 cup mixed nuts and seeds (almonds, walnuts, chia seeds, flaxseeds)
- ☐ 1/2 cup mixed berries
- ☐ 1 tablespoon honey (optional)

Instructions:

1. In a glass or bowl, layer Greek yogurt, mixed nuts and seeds, and mixed berries.
2. Drizzle with honey if desired.
3. Mix well before consuming. Greek yogurt is a protein-rich food that helps control blood sugar levels, and the combination of nuts, seeds, and berries adds fiber and additional nutrients.

Avocado and Smoked Salmon Toast:

Ingredients:

- ☐ 1 slice whole grain bread (gluten-free if desired)
- ☐ 1/2 ripe avocado, mashed
- ☐ 2 ounces smoked salmon
- ☐ Lemon juice
- ☐ Salt and pepper to taste

Instructions:

1. Toast the bread until golden brown.
2. Spread the mashed avocado evenly on the toast.
3. Top with smoked salmon.
4. Squeeze lemon juice over the salmon and season with salt and pepper.
5. Enjoy this omega-3 fatty acid-rich breakfast that provides healthy fats, protein, and fiber, promoting stable blood sugar levels.

Overnight Chia Pudding:
Ingredients:
- 1/4 cup chia seeds
- 1 cup unsweetened almond milk
- 1/2 teaspoon vanilla extract
- 1 tablespoon sugar-free sweetener (stevia, erythritol)
- 1/4 cup mixed berries (optional topping)

Instructions:
1. In a jar or bowl, combine chia seeds, almond milk, vanilla extract, and sweetener.
2. Stir well to combine and ensure there are no lumps.
3. Cover and refrigerate overnight.

4. In the morning, give the mixture a good stir and add mixed berries on top if desired.
5. Chia seeds are high in fiber and can help slow down the absorption of sugar, making this pudding a great option for those with insulin resistance.
6. Note: It's important to consult with a healthcare professional or registered dietitian before making any significant changes to your diet, especially if you have insulin resistance or any other medical condition.

Soup And Salad

Greek Salad with Grilled Chicken:
Ingredients:

- 2 cups mixed greens
- 1 cup cherry tomatoes, halved
- 1 cucumber, diced
- 1/2 red onion, thinly sliced
- 1/4 cup Kalamata olives, pitted and halved
- 4 ounces grilled chicken breast, sliced
- 2 tablespoons extra virgin olive oil
- 2 tablespoons lemon juice
- 1 teaspoon dried oregano

Salt and pepper to taste

Instructions:

1. In a large bowl, combine the mixed greens, cherry tomatoes, cucumber, red onion, and Kalamata olives. Add the grilled chicken slices on top. In a separate small bowl, whisk together the olive oil, lemon juice, dried oregano, salt, and pepper. Drizzle the dressing over the salad and toss gently to combine. Serve chilled.

Roasted Butternut Squash Soup:

Ingredients:

- [ ] 1 medium butternut squash, peeled and cubed
- [ ] 1 onion, chopped
- [ ] 2 carrots, chopped
- [ ] 2 cloves garlic, minced
- [ ] 4 cups vegetable broth
- [ ] 1 teaspoon ground cinnamon
- [ ] 1/2 teaspoon ground nutmeg
- [ ] Salt and pepper to taste
- [ ] 2 tablespoons olive oil

Instructions:

1. Preheat the oven to 400°F (200°C). Place the cubed butternut squash on a baking sheet and drizzle with olive oil. Season with salt, pepper, and half of the ground cinnamon. Roast in the oven for 25-30 minutes until tender and lightly browned. In a large pot, heat the olive oil over medium heat. Add the chopped onion, carrots, and garlic, and sauté until the vegetables are softened. Add the roasted butternut squash to the pot, along with the vegetable broth, remaining ground cinnamon, and nutmeg. Bring to a boil, then reduce the heat and simmer for 15 minutes. Use an immersion blender or regular blender to puree the soup until smooth. Season with additional salt and pepper if needed. Serve hot.

Quinoa and Kale Soup:
Ingredients:
- ☐ 1 cup cooked quinoa
- ☐ 2 cups kale, chopped
- ☐ 1 onion, diced
- ☐ 2 carrots, diced
- ☐ 2 celery stalks, diced
- ☐ 3 cloves garlic, minced
- ☐ 4 cups vegetable broth

- [ ] 1 teaspoon dried thyme
- [ ] 1 teaspoon paprika
- [ ] Salt and pepper to taste
- [ ] 2 tablespoons olive oil

Instructions:

1. Heat the olive oil in a large pot over medium heat. Add the diced onion, carrots, celery, and minced garlic. Sauté until the vegetables are tender. Add the kale to the pot and cook until wilted. Pour in the vegetable broth, cooked quinoa, dried thyme, paprika, salt, and pepper. Bring the soup to a boil, then reduce the heat and simmer for 15-20 minutes. Adjust the seasonings if needed. Serve hot.

Spinach and Mushroom Salad:
Ingredients:
- [ ] 4 cups baby spinach
- [ ] 1 cup sliced mushrooms
- [ ] 1/4 cup sliced red onion
- [ ] 1/4 cup crumbled feta cheese
- [ ] 2 tablespoons balsamic vinegar
- [ ] 2 tablespoons extra virgin olive oil
- [ ] 1 tablespoon Dijon mustard
- [ ] Salt and pepper to taste

Instructions:

1. In a large bowl, combine the baby spinach, sliced mushrooms, red onion, and crumbled feta cheese. In a separate small bowl, whisk together the balsamic vinegar, olive oil, Dijon mustard, salt, and pepper. Drizzle the dressing over the salad and toss gently to coat. Serve immediately.

2.

Lentil and Vegetable Soup:

Ingredients:

- □ 1 cup dried lentils, rinsed and drained
- □ 1 onion, chopped
- □ 2 carrots, diced
- □ 2 celery stalks, diced
- □ 2 cloves garlic, minced
- □ 4 cups vegetable broth
- □ 1 can diced tomatoes
- □ 1 teaspoon ground cumin
- □ 1/2 teaspoon turmeric powder
- □ Salt and pepper to taste
- □ 2 tablespoons olive oil

Instructions:

1. Heat the olive oil in a large pot over medium heat. Add the chopped onion, carrots, celery, and minced garlic. Sauté until the vegetables are softened. Add the rinsed lentils, vegetable broth, diced tomatoes (with juice), ground cumin, turmeric powder, salt, and pepper. Bring the soup to a boil, then reduce the heat and simmer for 25-30 minutes until the lentils are tender. Adjust the seasonings if needed. Serve hot.

Avocado and Tomato Salad:
Ingredients:
- ☐ 2 ripe avocados, diced
- ☐ 1 cup cherry tomatoes, halved
- ☐ 1/4 cup chopped fresh cilantro
- ☐ 2 tablespoons lime juice
- ☐ 1 tablespoon extra virgin olive oil
- ☐ 1 clove garlic, minced
- ☐ Salt and pepper to taste

Instructions:
1. In a bowl, combine the diced avocados, cherry tomatoes, and chopped cilantro. In a separate small bowl, whisk together the lime juice, olive oil, minced garlic, salt, and pepper. Drizzle the

dressing over the salad and gently toss to
combine. Serve immediately.

Lunch

Quinoa Salad with Grilled Chicken and Veggies:
Ingredients:
- 1 cup cooked quinoa
- 4 ounces grilled chicken breast, sliced
- 1 cup mixed vegetables (bell peppers, zucchini, broccoli)
- 2 tablespoons olive oil
- 1 tablespoon lemon juice
- 1 teaspoon Dijon mustard
- Salt and pepper to taste

Instructions:
1. In a large bowl, combine cooked quinoa, grilled chicken, and mixed vegetables.
2. In a separate small bowl, whisk together olive oil, lemon juice, Dijon mustard, salt, and pepper.
3. Pour the dressing over the quinoa mixture and toss to coat evenly. Serve chilled.

Baked Salmon with Roasted Vegetables:

Ingredients:

- 4 ounces salmon fillet
- 1 cup mixed roasted vegetables (broccoli, cauliflower, carrots)
- 1 tablespoon olive oil
- 1 teaspoon dried herbs (such as thyme or rosemary)
- Salt and pepper to taste

Instructions:

1. Preheat the oven to 400°F (200°C). Place the salmon fillet on a baking sheet lined with parchment paper.
2. In a separate bowl, toss the mixed vegetables with olive oil, dried herbs, salt, and pepper.
3. Spread the seasoned vegetables around the salmon on the baking sheet.
4. Bake for about 15-20 minutes, or until the salmon is cooked through and the vegetables are tender. Serve hot.

Turkey Lettuce Wraps:

Ingredients:

- 4 large lettuce leaves (such as romaine or iceberg)
- 8 ounces ground turkey
- 1/2 cup diced bell peppers
- 1/4 cup diced onions
- 1 clove garlic, minced
- 1 tablespoon low-sodium soy sauce
- 1 teaspoon sesame oil
- 1/2 teaspoon ground ginger
- Salt and pepper to taste

Instructions:

1. Heat a skillet over medium heat and cook the ground turkey until browned and cooked through.
2. Add the diced bell peppers, onions, and garlic to the skillet and sauté for a few minutes until tender.
3. In a small bowl, whisk together soy sauce, sesame oil, ground ginger, salt, and pepper. Pour the sauce over the turkey mixture and stir to combine.
4. Spoon the turkey mixture onto the lettuce leaves and roll them up tightly. Serve as wraps.

Chickpea and Vegetable Stir-Fry:

Ingredients:

- ☐ 1 can (15 ounces) chickpeas, drained and rinsed
- ☐ 1 cup mixed vegetables (broccoli, bell peppers, carrots, snow peas)
- ☐ 2 tablespoons olive oil
- ☐ 2 cloves garlic, minced
- ☐ 1 teaspoon grated fresh ginger
- ☐ 2 tablespoons low-sodium soy sauce
- ☐ 1 tablespoon honey or maple syrup (optional)
- ☐ Salt and pepper to taste

Instructions:

1. Heat olive oil in a large skillet over medium-high heat. Add garlic and ginger and sauté for about 1 minute until fragrant.
2. Add the mixed vegetables and stir-fry for 3-4 minutes until slightly tender.
3. Add the chickpeas to the skillet and stir-fry for an additional 2 minutes.
4. In a small bowl, whisk together soy sauce, honey or maple syrup (optional), salt, and pepper. Pour the sauce over the chickpea and vegetable mixture and stir to combine. Cook for another minute until heated through. Serve hot.

Greek Salad with Grilled Shrimp:

Ingredients:

- ☐ 4 ounces grilled shrimp
- ☐ 2 cups mixed salad greens
- ☐ 1/2 cup cherry tomatoes, halved
- ☐ 1/4 cup sliced cucumber
- ☐ 1/4 cup sliced red onions
- ☐ 2 tablespoons crumbled feta cheese
- ☐ 2 tablespoons extra virgin olive oil
- ☐ 1 tablespoon lemon juice
- ☐ 1 teaspoon dried oregano
- ☐ Salt and pepper to taste

Instructions:

1. In a large bowl, combine the mixed salad greens, cherry tomatoes, cucumber, red onions, and feta cheese.
2. In a small bowl, whisk together olive oil, lemon juice, dried oregano, salt, and pepper.
3. Pour the dressing over the salad mixture and toss to coat evenly. Top with grilled shrimp. Serve chilled.

Lentil Soup with Spinach:

Ingredients:

- ☐ 1 cup dried green lentils
- ☐ 4 cups vegetable broth
- ☐ 1 cup chopped spinach
- ☐ 1 small onion, diced
- ☐ 2 cloves garlic, minced
- ☐ 1 carrot, diced
- ☐ 1 celery stalk, diced
- ☐ 1 teaspoon ground cumin
- ☐ 1/2 teaspoon ground turmeric
- ☐ Salt and pepper to taste

Instructions:

1. Rinse the lentils under cold water and drain. Set aside.
2. In a large pot, sauté the onion, garlic, carrot, and celery over medium heat until softened.
3. Add the lentils, vegetable broth, ground cumin, ground turmeric, salt, and pepper to the pot. Bring to a boil, then reduce heat and simmer for about 30-40 minutes until the lentils are tender.
4. Stir in the chopped spinach and cook for an additional 5 minutes until wilted. Adjust the seasoning if necessary. Serve hot.

Snacks And Sides

Roasted Chickpeas:

Ingredients:

- ☐ 1 can of chickpeas, drained and rinsed
- ☐ 1 tablespoon olive oil
- ☐ 1 teaspoon ground cumin
- ☐ 1/2 teaspoon paprika
- ☐ 1/2 teaspoon garlic powder
- ☐ Salt and pepper to taste

Instructions:

1. Preheat the oven to 400°F (200°C).

2. Pat the chickpeas dry with a paper towel and remove any loose skins.

3. In a bowl, combine the chickpeas, olive oil, cumin, paprika, garlic powder, salt, and pepper. Toss until the chickpeas are well coated.

4. Spread the chickpeas in a single layer on a baking sheet.

5. Roast in the oven for 25-30 minutes, or until the chickpeas are crispy and golden brown.

6. Remove from the oven and let them cool before serving. Enjoy as a crunchy and fiber-rich snack!

Baked Zucchini Fries:
Ingredients:
- ☐ 2 medium zucchinis, cut into fries
- ☐ 1/2 cup almond flour
- ☐ 1/2 cup grated Parmesan cheese
- ☐ 1 teaspoon dried Italian seasoning
- ☐ 1/2 teaspoon garlic powder
- ☐ Salt and pepper to taste
- ☐ 2 large eggs, beaten

Instructions:
1. Preheat the oven to 425°F (220°C). Line a baking sheet with parchment paper.

2. In a shallow bowl, mix together the almond flour, Parmesan cheese, Italian seasoning, garlic powder, salt, and pepper.
3. Dip each zucchini fry into the beaten eggs, then coat it with the almond flour mixture.
4. Place the coated fries on the prepared baking sheet in a single layer.

5. Bake for 15-20 minutes, or until the fries are golden and crispy.
6. Remove from the oven and let them cool slightly before serving. Serve with a side of sugar-free marinara sauce or a low-fat yogurt dip.

Greek Yogurt and Berry Parfait:
Ingredients:
- ☐ 1 cup plain Greek yogurt
- ☐ 1/2 cup mixed berries (strawberries, blueberries, raspberries)
- ☐ 2 tablespoons chopped nuts (almonds, walnuts, or pistachios)
- ☐ 1 teaspoon honey (optional)

Instructions:
1. In a glass or bowl, layer the Greek yogurt, mixed berries, and chopped nuts.

2. Drizzle honey over the top if desired.
3. Repeat the layers until all the ingredients are used.
4. Serve immediately or refrigerate for later. This parfait is packed with protein, fiber, and antioxidants.

Cucumber and Tomato Salad:

Ingredients:

- ☐ 2 medium cucumbers, thinly sliced
- ☐ 2 medium tomatoes, diced
- ☐ 1/4 red onion, thinly sliced
- ☐ 2 tablespoons chopped fresh parsley
- ☐ 2 tablespoons extra virgin olive oil
- ☐ 1 tablespoon lemon juice
- ☐ Salt and pepper to taste

Instructions:

1. In a large bowl, combine the sliced cucumbers, diced tomatoes, red onion, and fresh parsley.
2. In a small bowl, whisk together the olive oil, lemon juice, salt, and pepper.
3. Pour the dressing over the cucumber and tomato mixture. Toss gently to combine.
4. Let the salad marinate in the refrigerator for at least 30 minutes before serving. It's a refreshing and low-carb side dish.

Baked Sweet Potato Chips:

Ingredients:

- ☐ 2 medium sweet potatoes, peeled
- ☐ 1 tablespoon olive oil

- □ 1 teaspoon smoked paprika
- □ 1/2 teaspoon garlic powder
- □ Salt to taste

Instructions:
1. Preheat the oven to 375°F (190°C). Line a baking sheet with parchment paper.
2. Using a mandoline or a sharp knife, slice the sweet potatoes into thin rounds.
3. In a bowl, toss the sweet potato slices with olive oil, smoked paprika, garlic powder, and salt.
4. Arrange the slices in a single layer on the prepared baking sheet.
5. Bake for 15-20 minutes, or until the chips are crispy and slightly golden.
6. Allow them to cool completely before serving. Enjoy as a healthier alternative to traditional potato chips.

Avocado and Tomato Salsa:
Ingredients:
- □ 2 ripe avocados, diced
- □ 2 medium tomatoes, diced
- □ 1/4 red onion, finely chopped
- □ 1 small jalapeño, seeded and finely chopped

- 2 tablespoons chopped fresh cilantro
- 1 tablespoon lime juice
- Salt and pepper to taste

Instructions:

1. In a bowl, combine the diced avocados, tomatoes, red onion, jalapeño, and cilantro.
2. Drizzle the lime juice over the mixture and gently toss to combine.
3. Season with salt and pepper to taste.
4. Allow the flavors to meld by refrigerating for at least 30 minutes before serving.
5. Serve with whole-grain tortilla chips or as a topping for grilled chicken or fish.
6. These recipes provide a range of flavors and textures while adhering to an insulin resistance diet plan. Enjoy these delicious and nutritious snacks and sides!

Vegetarian And Vegan Entrees

Quinoa-Stuffed Bell Peppers:
Ingredients:

- 4 bell peppers (any color)

- [ ] 1 cup cooked quinoa
- [ ] 1 cup black beans, drained and rinsed
- [ ] 1 cup diced tomatoes
- [ ] 1/2 cup corn kernels
- [ ] 1/2 cup diced onions
- [ ] 1/2 cup diced zucchini
- [ ] 2 cloves garlic, minced
- [ ] 1 teaspoon cumin
- [ ] 1 teaspoon paprika
- [ ] Salt and pepper to taste

Instructions:

1. Preheat the oven to 375°F (190°C). Cut the tops off the bell peppers and remove the seeds.
2. In a large skillet, sauté the onions, garlic, and zucchini until softened.
3. Add the cooked quinoa, black beans, diced tomatoes, and corn kernels to the skillet. Stir in the cumin, paprika, salt, and pepper.
4. Fill the bell peppers with the quinoa mixture and place them in a baking dish. Cover with foil and bake for 25-30 minutes.
5. Remove the foil and bake for an additional 5 minutes to allow the tops to brown slightly. Serve hot.

Lentil Curry:

Ingredients:

- ☐ 1 cup red lentils
- ☐ 1 onion, diced
- ☐ 2 cloves garlic, minced
- ☐ 1 tablespoon curry powder
- ☐ 1 teaspoon turmeric
- ☐ 1 teaspoon cumin
- ☐ 1 can (14 oz) coconut milk
- ☐ 1 cup vegetable broth
- ☐ 1 cup diced tomatoes
- ☐ 2 cups spinach leaves
- ☐ Salt and pepper to taste

Instructions:

1. Rinse the lentils under cold water and drain.
2. In a large pot, sauté the onions and garlic until translucent.
3. Add the lentils, curry powder, turmeric, and cumin to the pot and stir well.
4. Pour in the coconut milk, vegetable broth, and diced tomatoes. Bring to a boil, then reduce heat and simmer for about 20 minutes, or until lentils are tender.

5. Stir in the spinach leaves and cook until wilted. Season with salt and pepper.

6. Serve the lentil curry over brown rice or with whole grain bread.

Zucchini Noodles with Avocado Pesto:
Ingredients:
- 3 medium zucchini, spiralized
- 1 ripe avocado
- 1 cup fresh basil leaves
- 1/4 cup pine nuts
- 2 cloves garlic, minced
- Juice of 1 lemon
- 2 tablespoons nutritional yeast
- Salt and pepper to taste

Instructions:
1. In a blender or food processor, combine the avocado, basil leaves, pine nuts, garlic, lemon juice, nutritional yeast, salt, and pepper. Blend until smooth and creamy.
2. Spiralize the zucchini into noodle-like strands and place them in a large bowl.
3. Pour the avocado pesto over the zucchini noodles and toss until well coated.

4. Serve immediately or refrigerate for a couple of hours to allow the flavors to meld.

Chickpea and Vegetable Stir-Fry:
Ingredients:
- ☐ 1 can (15 oz) chickpeas, drained and rinsed
- ☐ 1 cup broccoli florets
- ☐ 1 cup sliced bell peppers
- ☐ 1 cup sliced mushrooms
- ☐ 1 cup snap peas
- ☐ 1/2 cup shredded carrots
- ☐ 2 cloves garlic, minced
- ☐ 2 tablespoons low-sodium soy sauce
- ☐ 1 tablespoon sesame oil
- ☐ 1 teaspoon grated ginger
- ☐ Salt and pepper to taste

Instructions:
1. In a large skillet or wok, heat the sesame oil over medium heat. Add the garlic and grated ginger and cook for 1-2 minutes.
2. Add the broccoli, bell peppers, mushrooms, snap peas, and carrots to the skillet. Stir-fry for about 5 minutes or until the vegetables are tender-crisp.

3. Stir in the chickpeas and cook for an additional 2-3 minutes.
4. Pour the soy sauce over the stir-fry and toss to coat the vegetables and chickpeas. Season with salt and pepper.
5. Remove from heat and serve the stir-fry over brown rice or quinoa.

Sweet Potato and Black Bean Enchiladas:
Ingredients:
- 4 medium sweet potatoes, peeled and cubed
- 1 can (15 oz) black beans, drained and rinsed
- 1 cup diced onions
- 2 cloves garlic, minced
- 1 teaspoon chili powder
- 1/2 teaspoon cumin
- 8 whole wheat tortillas
- 1 cup enchilada sauce
- 1/2 cup shredded vegan cheese (optional)
- Fresh cilantro for garnish

Instructions:
1. Preheat the oven to 375°F (190°C). Boil the sweet potatoes until tender, then drain and mash.

2. In a large skillet, sauté the onions and garlic until softened. Add the black beans, chili powder, and cumin. Cook for a few minutes to combine the flavors.
3. Spread a thin layer of enchilada sauce on the bottom of a baking dish.
4. Fill each tortilla with a scoop of mashed sweet potatoes and a spoonful of the black bean mixture. Roll up the tortillas and place them seam side down in the baking dish.
5. Pour the remaining enchilada sauce over the rolled tortillas and sprinkle with vegan cheese, if desired.
6. Bake for 20-25 minutes, or until the enchiladas are heated through and the cheese is melted. Garnish with fresh cilantro before serving.

Mediterranean Quinoa Salad:
Ingredients:
- 1 cup cooked quinoa
- 1 cup cherry tomatoes, halved
- 1/2 cup diced cucumbers
- 1/2 cup diced red bell peppers
- 1/4 cup diced red onions
- 1/4 cup Kalamata olives, pitted and halved
- 2 tablespoons chopped fresh parsley

- ☐ Juice of 1 lemon
- ☐ 2 tablespoons extra virgin olive oil
- ☐ Salt and pepper to taste

Instructions:
1. In a large bowl, combine the cooked quinoa, cherry tomatoes, cucumbers, red bell peppers, red onions, and Kalamata olives.
2. In a small bowl, whisk together the lemon juice, olive oil, salt, and pepper.
3. Pour the dressing over the quinoa mixture and toss until well combined.
4. Sprinkle the chopped parsley on top and refrigerate for at least 30 minutes to allow the flavors to meld.
5. Serve chilled as a refreshing and nutritious salad.
6. These recipes provide a range of flavors and textures, ensuring a satisfying and healthy experience while following an insulin resistance diet plan. Enjoy!

Fish And Seafood Entrees

Baked Salmon with Lemon and Dill:

Ingredients:

- 4 salmon fillets (6 ounces each)
- 2 lemons, thinly sliced
- 2 tablespoons fresh dill, chopped
- 2 tablespoons olive oil
- Salt and pepper to taste

Instructions:

1. Preheat the oven to 400°F (200°C).
2. Place the salmon fillets on a baking sheet lined with parchment paper.
3. Season the fillets with salt and pepper, then drizzle with olive oil.
4. Arrange the lemon slices on top of the fillets and sprinkle with fresh dill.
5. Bake for 12-15 minutes or until the salmon is cooked through and flakes easily with a fork.
6. Serve with steamed vegetables or a side salad for a complete meal.

Grilled Shrimp Skewers with Vegetables:

Ingredients:

- 1 pound large shrimp, peeled and deveined
- 1 red bell pepper, cut into chunks
- 1 yellow bell pepper, cut into chunks
- 1 zucchini, sliced into rounds

- ☐ 1 red onion, cut into wedges
- ☐ 2 tablespoons olive oil
- ☐ 2 garlic cloves, minced
- ☐ 1 teaspoon paprika
- ☐ Salt and pepper to taste

Instructions:
1. Preheat the grill to medium-high heat.
2. In a large bowl, combine the shrimp, bell peppers, zucchini, red onion, olive oil, garlic, paprika, salt, and pepper.
3. Thread the shrimp and vegetables onto skewers, alternating between them.
4. Grill the skewers for 2-3 minutes per side, until the shrimp are pink and cooked through.
5. Remove from the grill and serve immediately. Enjoy with a squeeze of fresh lemon juice.

Tuna Avocado Lettuce Wraps:
Ingredients:
- ☐ 2 cans of tuna, drained
- ☐ 1 ripe avocado, mashed
- ☐ 2 tablespoons Greek yogurt
- ☐ 1 tablespoon lemon juice
- ☐ 2 tablespoons red onion, finely chopped
- ☐ Salt and pepper to taste

- Lettuce leaves for wrapping

Instructions:
1. In a medium bowl, combine the tuna, mashed avocado, Greek yogurt, lemon juice, red onion, salt, and pepper.
2. Mix well until all the ingredients are evenly incorporated.
3. Spoon the tuna mixture onto individual lettuce leaves and wrap them up.
4. Serve as a light and refreshing lunch or dinner option. You can also add sliced cucumber or tomato for extra crunch.

Cod with Roasted Vegetables:
Ingredients:
- 4 cod fillets (6 ounces each)
- 2 cups cherry tomatoes
- 2 cups asparagus spears
- 1 tablespoon olive oil
- 2 cloves garlic, minced
- 1 teaspoon dried oregano
- Salt and pepper to taste

Instructions:
1. Preheat the oven to 425°F (220°C).

2. Arrange the cod fillets, cherry tomatoes, and asparagus on a baking sheet.
3. Drizzle with olive oil and sprinkle with minced garlic, dried oregano, salt, and pepper.
4. Roast for 12-15 minutes or until the cod is cooked through and flakes easily.
5. Serve the cod on top of the roasted vegetables for a wholesome and flavorful meal.

Garlic Butter Scallops with Cauliflower Rice:
Ingredients:
- 1 pound scallops
- 2 tablespoons unsalted butter
- 3 cloves garlic, minced
- 1 tablespoon fresh parsley, chopped
- Salt and pepper to taste
- 4 cups cauliflower rice

Instructions:
1. Pat the scallops dry with a paper towel and season with salt and pepper.
2. In a large skillet, melt the butter over medium heat. Add the minced garlic and cook until fragrant.
3. Add the scallops to the skillet and cook for 2-3 minutes per side until golden brown.

4. Sprinkle the scallops with fresh parsley and remove them from the skillet.

5. In the same skillet, add the cauliflower rice and cook for 4-5 minutes until tender.

6. Serve the garlic butter scallops over a bed of cauliflower rice for a low-carb and satisfying meal.

Spicy Thai Coconut Shrimp Curry:
Ingredients:
- ☐ 1 pound shrimp, peeled and deveined
- ☐ 1 tablespoon coconut oil
- ☐ 1 onion, diced
- ☐ 2 cloves garlic, minced
- ☐ 1 red bell pepper, sliced
- ☐ 1 cup broccoli florets
- ☐ 1 can coconut milk
- ☐ 2 tablespoons Thai red curry paste
- ☐ 1 tablespoon fish sauce
- ☐ 1 tablespoon lime juice
- ☐ Fresh cilantro for garnish

Instructions:
1. In a large skillet, heat the coconut oil over medium heat. Add the diced onion and minced garlic, and sauté until fragrant.

2. Add the red bell pepper and broccoli florets to the skillet and cook for a few minutes until slightly tender.
3. Stir in the coconut milk, Thai red curry paste, fish sauce, and lime juice. Bring the mixture to a simmer.
4. Add the shrimp to the skillet and cook for 4-5 minutes or until they turn pink and opaque.
5. Serve the spicy Thai coconut shrimp curry over steamed cauliflower rice or with a side of quinoa. Garnish with fresh cilantro leaves.

Poultry And Meats Entrees

- Lemon Garlic Grilled Chicken:
- Ingredients:
- 4 boneless, skinless chicken breasts
- 2 lemons, juiced and zested
- 4 cloves of garlic, minced
- 2 tablespoons olive oil
- Salt and pepper to taste

Instructions:

1. In a bowl, whisk together the lemon juice, lemon zest, minced garlic, olive oil, salt, and pepper.

2. Add the chicken breasts to a resealable plastic bag and pour the marinade over them. Seal the bag and massage the marinade into the chicken. Marinate in the refrigerator for at least 30 minutes.

3. Preheat the grill to medium-high heat. Remove the chicken from the marinade, allowing any excess to drip off.

4. Grill the chicken for about 6-8 minutes per side, or until it reaches an internal temperature of 165°F (74°C).

5. Remove from the grill and let it rest for a few minutes before serving. Serve with steamed vegetables or a side salad.

Turkey and Vegetable Stir-Fry:
Ingredients:
- 1 lb (450g) turkey breast, sliced into thin strips
- 2 tablespoons low-sodium soy sauce
- 2 tablespoons olive oil
- 1 teaspoon minced ginger
- 2 cloves of garlic, minced
- 1 red bell pepper, thinly sliced
- 1 cup broccoli florets
- 1 cup snap peas
- 1 medium carrot, julienned

- ☐ Salt and pepper to taste

Instructions:
1. In a bowl, marinate the turkey breast strips in soy sauce for about 15 minutes.
2. Heat olive oil in a large skillet or wok over medium-high heat. Add minced ginger and garlic, stirring for about 30 seconds until fragrant.
3. Add the marinated turkey to the skillet and cook until browned, about 5-6 minutes.
4. Add the bell pepper, broccoli, snap peas, and carrot to the skillet. Stir-fry for about 4-5 minutes, until the vegetables are crisp-tender.
5. Season with salt and pepper to taste. Serve the stir-fry hot over cauliflower rice or quinoa.

Baked Salmon with Herbs:
Ingredients:
- ☐ 4 salmon fillets
- ☐ 2 tablespoons fresh dill, chopped
- ☐ 2 tablespoons fresh parsley, chopped
- ☐ 2 tablespoons fresh lemon juice
- ☐ 1 tablespoon olive oil
- ☐ Salt and pepper to taste

Instructions:

1. Preheat the oven to 375°F (190°C). Line a baking sheet with parchment paper.
2. Place the salmon fillets on the prepared baking sheet. Drizzle with lemon juice and olive oil. Season with salt and pepper.
3. Sprinkle the chopped dill and parsley evenly over the salmon fillets.
4. Bake for about 12-15 minutes, or until the salmon is cooked through and flakes easily with a fork.
5. Remove from the oven and let it rest for a couple of minutes. Serve with steamed vegetables or a side salad.

Grilled Balsamic Glazed Pork Chops:
Ingredients:
- 4 boneless pork chops
- 1/4 cup balsamic vinegar
- 2 tablespoons low-sodium soy sauce
- 2 tablespoons honey
- 1 tablespoon Dijon mustard
- 2 cloves of garlic, minced
- Salt and pepper to taste

Instructions:

1. In a small bowl, whisk together the balsamic vinegar, soy sauce, honey, Dijon mustard, minced garlic, salt, and pepper.
2. Preheat the grill to medium-high heat. Season the pork chops with salt and pepper on both sides.
3. Grill the pork chops for about 4-5 minutes per side, brushing with the balsamic glaze during the last few minutes of cooking.
4. Remove from the grill and let them rest for a few minutes. Serve the pork chops with a side of roasted vegetables or a mixed green salad.

Spicy Mexican Chicken Skillet:
Ingredients:
- 1 lb (450g) boneless, skinless chicken breasts, cut into strips
- 1 tablespoon olive oil
- 1 red bell pepper, sliced
- 1 green bell pepper, sliced
- 1 small red onion, sliced
- 1 jalapeño pepper, seeds removed and finely chopped
- 2 teaspoons chili powder
- 1 teaspoon ground cumin
- 1/2 teaspoon paprika

- ☐ 1/2 teaspoon garlic powder
- ☐ Salt and pepper to taste
- ☐ Fresh cilantro, chopped (for garnish)

Instructions:

1. Heat olive oil in a large skillet over medium-high heat. Add the chicken strips and cook until browned, about 4-5 minutes.

2. Add the sliced bell peppers, red onion, and jalapeño pepper to the skillet. Sauté for another 4-5 minutes until the vegetables are slightly softened.

3. In a small bowl, mix together the chili powder, cumin, paprika, garlic powder, salt, and pepper. Sprinkle the spice mixture over the chicken and vegetables in the skillet. Stir well to coat evenly.

4. Reduce the heat to medium and continue cooking for another 4-5 minutes until the chicken is cooked through and the vegetables are tender.

5. Garnish with fresh chopped cilantro before serving. Serve the spicy Mexican chicken skillet with cauliflower rice or whole grain tortillas.

Herb-Roasted Turkey Breast:

Ingredients:

- ☐ 2 lbs (900g) boneless turkey breast
- ☐ 2 tablespoons olive oil
- ☐ 1 tablespoon fresh rosemary, chopped
- ☐ 1 tablespoon fresh thyme, chopped
- ☐ 1 tablespoon fresh sage, chopped
- ☐ 2 cloves of garlic, minced
- ☐ Salt and pepper to taste

Instructions:

1. Preheat the oven to 375°F (190°C). Place the turkey breast in a roasting pan or a baking dish.
2. In a small bowl, combine the olive oil, chopped rosemary, thyme, sage, minced garlic, salt, and pepper.
3. Rub the herb mixture all over the turkey breast, making sure it is evenly coated.
4. Roast the turkey breast in the preheated oven for about 60-70 minutes, or until the internal temperature reaches 165°F (74°C).
5. Remove from the oven and let it rest for 10-15 minutes before slicing. Serve the herb-roasted turkey breast with a side of steamed vegetables or a fresh salad.

Drinks And Desserts

Chia Pudding

Ingredients:

- ☐ 2 tablespoons chia seeds
- ☐ 1 cup unsweetened almond milk
- ☐ 1/2 teaspoon vanilla extract
- ☐ 1/2 teaspoon cinnamon
- ☐ 1/4 cup fresh berries (blueberries, raspberries, or strawberries)

Instructions:

1. In a bowl, combine chia seeds, almond milk, vanilla extract, and cinnamon.
2. Stir well to evenly distribute the chia seeds. Let it sit for 10 minutes, stirring occasionally.
3. Transfer the mixture into individual serving cups and refrigerate for at least 2 hours or overnight.
4. Before serving, top with fresh berries. Enjoy this fiber-rich dessert!

Green Smoothie

Ingredients:

- ☐ 1 cup spinach
- ☐ 1/2 cucumber, peeled and chopped

- ☐ 1 small green apple, cored and chopped
- ☐ 1/2 lemon, juiced
- ☐ 1/2 cup unsweetened coconut water

Instructions:

1. In a blender, combine spinach, cucumber, green apple, lemon juice, and coconut water.
2.
3. Blend until smooth and creamy. If needed, add a little more coconut water to reach the desired consistency.
4. Pour into a glass and serve chilled. This refreshing green smoothie is packed with nutrients and helps stabilize blood sugar levels.

Sugar-Free Berry Lemonade
Ingredients:

- ☐ 1 cup fresh or frozen mixed berries (strawberries, raspberries, blueberries)
- ☐ Juice of 2 lemons
- ☐ 4 cups water
- ☐ Stevia or any sugar substitute, to taste
- ☐ Ice cubes

Instructions:

1. In a blender, combine the mixed berries, lemon juice, and 1 cup of water.
2. Blend until smooth. You can strain the mixture to remove any seeds, if desired.
3. In a pitcher, mix the berry mixture, remaining water, and sugar substitute. Adjust the sweetness according to your taste.
4. Add ice cubes and refrigerate until chilled. Serve this vibrant and tangy lemonade for a refreshing treat.

Baked Apple Slices
Ingredients:
- ☐ 2 medium apples, cored and sliced
- ☐ 1 tablespoon melted coconut oil
- ☐ 1 teaspoon ground cinnamon
- ☐ 1/4 teaspoon nutmeg (optional)
- ☐ 1 tablespoon chopped walnuts (optional)

Instructions:
1. Preheat the oven to 350°F (175°C) and line a baking sheet with parchment paper.
2. In a bowl, toss the apple slices with melted coconut oil, cinnamon, nutmeg (if using), and walnuts (if using).

3. Arrange the apple slices in a single layer on the prepared baking sheet.
4. Bake for about 20-25 minutes or until the apples are tender and slightly caramelized.
5. Remove from the oven and let them cool slightly. Enjoy these warm and spiced baked apple slices as a delightful dessert.

Cucumber Mint Infused Water
Ingredients:
- 1 medium cucumber, sliced
- 8-10 fresh mint leaves
- 4 cups water
- Ice cubes

Instructions:
1. In a pitcher, combine the cucumber slices, mint leaves, and water.
2. Stir well and refrigerate for at least 2 hours to allow the flavors to infuse.
3. Add ice cubes before serving. This refreshing infused water helps hydrate and supports a healthy insulin response.

Recipe: Chocolate Avocado Mousse
Ingredients:

- 1 ripe avocado, pitted and peeled
- 3 tablespoons unsweetened cocoa powder
- 2 tablespoons unsweetened almond milk
- 2 tablespoons sugar-free sweetener (such as stevia or erythritol)
- 1/2 teaspoon vanilla extract
- Pinch of sea salt

Instructions:

1. In a blender or food processor, combine the avocado, cocoa powder, almond milk, sweetener, vanilla extract, and sea salt.
2. Blend until smooth and creamy, scraping down the sides if needed.
3. Transfer the mousse into serving bowls or glasses.
4. Refrigerate for at least 30 minutes to allow the mousse to set.
5. Serve chilled and garnish with a sprinkle of cocoa powder or shaved dark chocolate. This rich and indulgent mousse is low in sugar and high in healthy fats.

CONCLUSION

As I reflect on the arduous journey of putting together the "Insulin Resistance Diet Plan Cookbook," I am filled with a sense of profound accomplishment. Crafting this book was no small feat, as it required countless hours of research, experimentation, and dedication. But now, as I hold the finished product in my hands, I can confidently say that it was all worth it.

The process of creating this cookbook was a labor of love. I delved deep into the intricate world of insulin resistance, meticulously examining the relationship between food and our bodies. From there, I embarked on a mission to design recipes that not only nourish the soul but also empower individuals to take control of their health.

Days turned into nights as I poured over scientific studies, consulted with nutritionists and medical professionals, and tested numerous ingredient combinations in my kitchen. There were moments of frustration when a recipe didn't turn out as planned or when I faced the daunting task of simplifying complex nutritional information. However, through it all, my unwavering determination pushed me forward.

With each recipe carefully crafted, I had a vision of the positive impact it could have on countless lives. I wanted to create a resource that not only provided delicious meals but also educated and inspired readers to make healthier choices. I wanted to empower individuals with insulin resistance to reclaim their health and regain control over their bodies.

Now, as the "Insulin Resistance Diet Plan Cookbook" reaches your hands, I implore you to take a moment to reflect on the journey that brought it to life. Every page represents countless hours of hard work, passion, and dedication. And now, I need your help.

Your support means everything to me. By dropping a review and sharing this book with your family and friends, you become a crucial part of the movement to spread awareness about insulin resistance and healthy living. Together, we can create a ripple effect of change, touching the lives of those who need it most.

So, I invite you to delve into the pages of this cookbook, savor the recipes, and experience the transformative power of nourishing your body with intention. Let the flavors dance on your taste buds, and let the knowledge within empower you to make informed decisions about your health.

Remember, this book is not just a collection of recipes; it is a culmination of my passion, expertise, and desire to make a difference. With your support, we can make an impact, one plate at a time.

Thank you for joining me on this incredible journey, and I eagerly await your reviews and shares. Together, we can help countless individuals embrace a healthier, more vibrant life.

Printed in Great Britain
by Amazon

46450702R00036